BEYOND THIS DARKNESS

BEYOND THIS DARKNESS

A Faith-Based Pathway to Recovery
from Addictive Behaviors

Ben Pugh, Jason Glover,
and Daniel Thompson

RESOURCE *Publications* · Eugene, Oregon

BEYOND THIS DARKNESS
A Faith-Based Pathway to Recovery from Addictive Behaviors

Resource Publications
An Imprint of Wipf and Stock Publishers
199 W. 8th Ave., Suite 3
Eugene, OR 97401

www.wipfandstock.com

PAPERBACK ISBN: 978-1-5326-1803-1
HARDCOVER ISBN: 978-1-4982-4323-0
EBOOK ISBN: 978-1-4982-4322-3

Manufactured in the U.S.A.   04/17/17

To: Everyone whose life has become a battle ground

CONTENTS

ACKNOWLEDGEMENTS

We would just like to acknowledge, first of all, the people that helped us along the path to recovery and to faith in Christ, without whom we might well not even be alive today.

Secondly, we would like to extend our thanks to all those that have helped to formulate this material through their encouragements and comments. In particular, we would like to mention Ricardo Lynch and Rev. Darren Howie, and the BA Theology students who were the members of Ben's Discipleship Group at Cliff College in 2016–17. They had a go at working the seven steps and made many helpful comments.

INTRODUCTION

W<small>HY DO SO MANY</small> of us get caught in "stinking thinking," and stuck in overwhelming urges that lead to bad behavior of one sort or another? We have thought about this long and hard. It seems to us to be a question of "culture" and "community."

Our ancestors lived in communities. That is to say, the vast majority of people lived in a village of only a few hundred people centered on church or chapel, on village hall and on the family dinner table and hearth. Everyone knew everyone else and there were few nuclear families. Mostly, there would be extended family all over the village. Perhaps a whole section of the village would be full of no-one but relatives of yours. You would inherit a family trade that had been passed down generations. You may have caught a whiff here and there of a wider culture: news of the royal family, or of a war, or of a new philosophical trend to sweep the great urban centers. But your own life would carry on much as before.

That was community. It had its drawbacks: even now, to live in a village is to accept prying and curiosity that may not always be welcome. In a community, your business is everyone's business, it just is. And in a community it is harder to break rules. Everyone is supposed to know their place and there can be bitter opposition to anything that threatens the status quo. But community also had its benefits. In community there is rarely anyone that has an "identity crisis" or who feels "insecure." There is a deep, deep sense of belonging, and of place. In a word, there is security. Security only exists when there is beneath us a sense of something permanent and reliable: a stable awareness that you will always be accepted just for who you are.

With the drift to the cities that came with industrialization, all that changed. Initially, the main impact felt by the new working classes was the de-humanizing effects of working in factories, no longer to the rhythms of sun and moon and the seasons of nature, but to the all-powerful clock. But even for the better off, the cities meant that community was increasingly becoming a distant memory or perhaps something that had never even been experienced. In its stead came culture. Culture replaced community in the urban-dominated, technological societies of the West. The result of that was partly quite superficial. The nineteenth century Danish philosopher Søren Kierkkegaard, who was born of such a wealthy family that he never needed to look for a job, commented penetratingly on the chattering classes that he mixed with in Copenhagen. They lived for the next concert, show, exhibition or ball. He described them as desiring only the aesthetic, as forever in pursuit of the next spectacle. Their main criterion was not, "Is this right or wrong?" but "Is this boring or exciting?"

There is, however, a more profound impact that the replacement of community by culture entails, and it affects all of us. It is this, that, while communities have expectations, these are limited and off-set by the unconditional sense of belonging that undergirds them, the family and tribal ties that ensure that one never ultimately needs to qualify for inclusion. Culture, on the other hand, is far more wide ranging and competitive. It is contributed to by artists, thinkers, newscasters, publishers, advertisers, playwrights, screenwriters and so on, who together give to the culture the thing that communities once had: normality. The culture decides for us what is normal and expected. The difficulties come when this culture is so vast it stretches across several continents, as this vast block of shared values that we call Western culture does. And it is in the nature of culture to monopolize and colonize everybody simply because it is naturally quick to master mass communication. Soon, hundreds of millions of people are all imbibing the same creative art forms and understanding themselves via the same TV channels and being kept supposedly "in touch" (another replacement for community) with what is going on in the world via the same news media. Everything that culture gives us is a substitute for what community once gave us. The stable sense of identity is replaced by an insatiable appetite for cultural artefacts: novels, films, art, music, shopping, fashion, different types of alcohol, and luxury foods. These now are our main sources of identity. We construct who we are out of the materials of what music we listen to, what clothes we buy, what cars we drive.

The overall effect of culture is that the stakes are raised too high. We need the approval and applause not of mere family members (such would be almost an insult) but of the culture, a culture that now spans several continents. And anything less than this will not do, simply because we don't have anything else to fall back on. We have become dependent on a vast autocratic culture that offers glamour and luxury beyond our craziest hopes if we will just believe in ourselves and follow our dream – and buy all its products along the way.

We expect to be successful and famous: why? Because of what we see modeled by the rich and famous. And we know that success came to these people because they were excessively self-centered. They pursued their dreams at the cost of family and friends, and at the cost of community. One former alcoholic and crack addict put it aptly:

> [Our culture rewards people who] are excessive. Absolutely. I mean, we don't find anyone who has grown up to achieve what we hold up to be the epitome of success in our society, who has balance. . .You don't become Tiger Woods by having balance.[1]

This is why one of the most crucial things that those of us who want to help can do is to provide community, community that helps put appropriate limits on our expectations of ourselves, soothing us with the warm embrace of unconditional acceptance.

1. Cited in Dann, *Addiction: Pastoral Responses*, 70.

Some of the very latest research into addiction supports the fact that, until community is provided in some way, we are only dealing with the symptoms and not the ultimate cause. The experiments consisted of adding cocaine to the water of a solitary rat in a cage, and having only plain water in the water bottle of the control animal. Sure, enough, very soon the rat drinking the doctored water developed an insatiable and obsessive desire for the cocaine. The rat just would not leave its water bottle alone. Within months, it had killed itself with cocaine use. And this experiment was repeated, producing the same result in 9 out of 10 cases, thus supposedly reinforcing the idea that addictions are just chemical and physiological. However, realizing that rats are sociable animals, a rather more enlightened scientist did things a bit differently. He too, had rats in individual cages drinking cocaine water but he also developed a rat utopia called Rat Park. Rat Park was a rat's paradise: a very pleasant outdoor location with plenty of space and, crucially, lots of other rats to socialize with. In Rat Park, some of the water bottles were laced with cocaine, some were not. Many of the rats sampled the cocaine water but not one of them became addicted. There was not one cocaine-related fatality. Then, the rats in the individual cages who, in their loneliness and boredom, had become thoroughly addicted, were released into Rat Park and began socializing with all the other rats. Some withdrawal symptoms were obvious: they got the shakes, but very soon they had detoxed and, even though cocaine continued to be freely available to all the rats in Rat Park, including the former addicts, there were no relapses. An article reporting on this is aptly titled: "It's not you, it's your cage."[2]

Humans are social creatures and are only ever complete in the context of community, which perhaps helps to explain the appeal of AA: it provides a meaningful and countercultural experience of community.

---

2. Michelle Amerman, "Addiction Is Not You, It's Your Cage." *Pathways* (Sep 23, 2015) [accessed online 28 Feb 2017] http://pathwaysreallife.com/addiction-you-its-cage/

Are You Addicted?

The scope of what we are calling the STAMP-IT-OUT[3] program is broad. The addiction stories we cite are principally drawn from four types of addiction: alcohol, drugs, gambling and porn. We know there are many other things people become addicted to besides these but we reckon that these four widely varying kinds of addiction can be taken as representative. And we feel excited that if we can identify the fundamental nature of all four of these, as well as point to the answers, then we have done that for all addictions.

We also think that very similar principles probably apply to eating disorders and self-harm but we recognize the limits of our expertise, so have not explicitly applied STAMP-IT-OUT to these. However, if you suffer in one or both of these ways and find this material helpful, we would love to hear from you.

One thing that is beyond the scope of this book is the medical issue of physical dependence on alcohol or drugs. It is a well-known fact that to suddenly come off alcohol if there is a serious physical dependence could lead to death. We heartily recommend an initial medical intervention and perhaps some time drying out in a rehab in cases of severe physical addiction. This book will then show the way to the spiritual answers that could lead to a new life.

It seems good to pause for a moment for some diagnostic discussion of addiction, not least because of fairly recent trends towards seeing everyone as an addict. We are, I hope, moving beyond hysterical ideas about an "addicted society" with its accompanying 12-Step Recovery epidemic which included everything from Artists Anonymous to Emotional Health Anonymous, to Ethics Anonymous to Workaholics Anonymous. Addictions proper would appear to include only a fairly small percentage of the population, though there is much, scientifically, that remains a mystery about it. Indeed, part of being able to help people who are addicts is the ability to accept the inexplicable, the amoral and

---

3. 1. Step Back, 2. Take Stock, 3. Acquire a New Master, 4. Make a Deep Connection, 5. Put Down the Lies, 6. Investigate the Urges, 7. Take the OUT Track.

irrational, and not to keep trying to make it make sense. "Addiction cannot be directed, issued ultimatums, threatened with hell or prison, or driven out. Addiction can only be loved."[4] It requires a skillful combination of "unqualified acceptance" and "straightforward feedback."[5]

There is, however, a key document, generally referred to as DSM IV,[6] which lays down seven signs of addiction. If a person presents with three or more of the following, they have an addiction:

1. Tolerance

2. Withdrawal

3. Exceeding Intentions

4. Relapse

5. Poor Use of Time

6. Interference

7. Problems Get Worse

Generally, an addiction or dependence in its early stages will look like 5–7. This early stage is called "abuse" because it is a level or type of use that has become obviously harmful to self and others and yet has been persisted in for at least one year. There are more and more signs of relationship strains, tensions with employers and even illegal activity such as theft. The substance abuser becomes less and less reliable because of the very time-consuming nature of thinking about, making arrangements for and recuperating from a binge. And, whatever mental or physical health problems or financial difficulties there might have been start to get considerably worse. Then, as the problem becomes an addiction,

4. Dann, *Addiction: Pastoral Responses*, 42.

5. Ibid., 53.

6 The *Diagnostic and Statistical Manual of Mental Disorders*. Available here: https://justines2010blog.files.wordpress.com/2011/03/dsm-iv.pdf [accessed 01/04/2015]. This has been superseded by DSM V and you are invited to compare it but DSM V, in its efforts to clarify statements made in DSM IV seems to have lost the simplicity of DSM IV.

more and more of points 1–4 become recognizable, yet this could be either a physical dependence, or an addiction proper, which includes physical and psychological causes. By the time the addict seeks help, they will already have tried many times to quit and will be stuck at point 4.

Dann describes graphically the power of addiction from the viewpoint of someone trying to help:

> . . . reasonable people want to shout, 'Just say no! 'Just don't do it.' They ask, 'What are you thinking?' 'Are you stupid?' 'Don't you care?' But the only answer is they are addicted. This powerlessness is what the term addiction truly means.[7]

Addictions tend to consume a person's life, they very soon cease to be pleasurable and they are marked by an apparent inability to choose *not* to do something.[8]

Despite the destructive nature of addictive behavior, many do not accept that they have a problem. David was a man who went to a treatment facility for cocaine, alcohol and designer drug use. He once described an occasion when he passed out on the floor in front of his seven year old daughter, and became momentarily paralyzed, yet he truly believed that this was not a problem. He did not believe he needed rehabilitation, and felt that society was trying to force him to change. He believed he was being persecuted for his personality and beliefs, as though the world was prejudiced against drug users. He could actually argue his point quite well to Daniel, who was trying to help. There were moments when David showed some signs of regret, especially when he thought of his daughter: he would have liked to have been able to protect her, but, in most conversations, he chose to defend his addictions instead.

This is often called "denial." The problem is that an addict cannot imagine life without his or her addictions. Many addicts have developed an addiction-centered outlook on life, and there is a very real fear of change. The addict will often have doubts but

7. Dann, *Addiction: Pastoral Responses*, 27.
8. Lenters, *The Freedom we Crave*, 62

they train themselves to not spend too much time reflecting on these doubts.

Pain will often be the thing that causes reality to dawn. Many recovery programs speak of hitting bottom, or rock-bottom. This is the point at which an addict has lost enough to consider changing. The experience of hitting bottom varies from sufferer to sufferer. One individual could recall his rock -bottom experience as the day he stole five pounds from his wife's purse, yet others do not experience it despite countless losses in all areas of life.

Many recovered addicts that Daniel has met can recognize a number of points in their lives when they have had an experience that caused them to consider recovery. One woman said that during every pregnancy of her seven children, she had a desperate desire to stop taking crack-cocaine. She said that each time she didn't, it broke her heart, and that if someone had approached her in those moments, she may have given recovery a try. In her eyes, she had a rock-bottom experience every day. The difficulty was that she was not given the opportunity to seize the moment. As sad as it seems, utilizing the pain of the last great failure can lead to some huge changes. Never waste pain.

Why are we not all addicts?

It is worth briefly considering the reverse side of the question about what an addiction is and to think about why, though exposed to many of the same pressures and temptations, we do not all become addicts. The answers hopefully reinforce what we have said and will say about the cures for addiction. We can say three things:

1. Non-addicts, though assailed by the same temptations have more inbuilt resistance to the notion that one particular thing could provide all the answers. They are not vulnerable, in other words, to obsession.

2. Non-addicts have a wide variety of sources of satisfaction in life, especially in relationships, and

3. Non-addicts have a healthy self-respect and sturdy self-esteem that enables them to fend off the "wolves of guilt and anxiety."[9]

Who Needs Another Recovery Program?

There are certainly plenty of resources out there for dealing with addictions: non-faith based resources such as SMART or AVRT, broadly faith-based 12 Steps, or explicitly Christian *Celebrate Recovery* and *Crossroads*. All of these are really helpful and we have used what we think are the best features of all of these and more. We like to think that the unique contributions this book makes are fourfold:

1. It includes the voice and experience of the addict more than most.

2. It draws widely from the latest research in addiction therapy rather than being dogmatic about a particular structure.

3. It is genuinely faith-based in that the original spark for the whole thing was Paul's letter to the Romans.

4. It seeks to cater for the whole range of addictive behaviors from chocolate to crack-cocaine.

Take one of these four elements and you do not have a unique program. Put them together and we think that leaves you with something very definitely worth a try.

A Word about Names

Nearly all the names you will read in this book are fictitious and have been made up to protect the identities of those whose stories you will read. There are two exceptions to this. One is if the story has come from a published work or website, in which case the author will usually have already gone public with their identity.

9. Lenters, *The Freedom we Crave*, 62.

These cases will be obvious as we always include a reference to any publications that are used. The other exception is when it is one of us, the three authors of this book, who is telling their story. In these cases, the book will refer to them in the third person using their first names: Ben, Jason or Daniel. There are no other Bens, Jasons or Daniels so you will always know it is one of us.

Our Disclaimer

Neither we, the authors, nor the publishers are making any claims to clinical expertise and we are not peddling this piece of work as a psychotherapeutic or medical intervention. It is a faith-based pathway to what we hope will be greater wholeness and freedom and we cannot accept any responsibility for any particular failure, real or apparent, that might be noted in the course of seeking to apply the insights offered. We would, however, welcome any constructive feedback as to how this program could work better.

How to Use this Book

If you are running an addictions group, it is advisable to obtain a copy for each participant but we do not have a set format as to how we think the book should be used. A suggestion is that the leader of the addictions group inwardly digests the material and delivers it in ten minute bursts interspersed by discussion. Good places to stop for discussion are indicated by our "Pause for Thought" headings, which also give a suggested discussion question. There would typically be two or three sections of teaching followed by a discussion. Then, at the end there might be a Scripture to look up and an action to perform. There are also biographical snippets which are there to reinforce the content and can be used in any way that seems appropriate.

Materials Needed

We advise that each participant obtain a notebook which will become their recovery journal. As the leader, you might choose to
supply everyone with one. In this they should regularly make notes
about their progress and about insights they gain along the way.
This could perhaps be brought along to each group and a session
might finish with an open invitation for any participant to share an
insight from their journal.

1

STEP BACK

A Situation that is Out of Control

IMAGINE YOU ARE A chariot rider in the races of ancient Rome.
You are in charge of your horses and you are good at what you do.

You have a quick mind and great judgment. You have two horses. One of the horses has always been a little easier to control than the other. This easier one represents your emotions and deep desires and fears. The more difficult horse is your appetitive side: that part of you that craves food, drink and sex. These appetites too easily become gluttony, drunkenness and lust. So, one horse can be controlled, albeit with some effort, but the other one keeps pulling away, threatening to take the chariot in the direction of your appetites.

Now imagine that the situation has got so out of control that, actually, neither of your horses is possible to control. Now it is a two-part struggle, a tug-of-war, if you like, between you, with your good sense of judgement, and the irrational passions and appetites that forever threaten to take you off in the wrong direction. Both your emotional life and your physical appetites are disordered. You may have been a champion chariot driver once but now no one is cheering from the sidelines. You have become a laughing stock, both horses charging this way and that.

The Apostle Paul used to call this irrational, appetitive side to us the "flesh." It includes both things: unhealthy emotions and physical urges. Paul saw the flesh as the powerhouse of all our uncontrolled passions and appetites. This is the situation you and I are up against as we contemplate, perhaps with a good deal of despair, the qualities and habits in our lives that seem unmanageable. Both horses have long been out of control. But there is hope. . .

Getting a Better View

The thing that will help us to begin with is to focus on the fact that this "flesh" aspect of our lives is not "you." It is not the inner, core you. The horses are out of control but there is still a driver who is still in the driving seat. You are not the horses: you are the driver. Paul himself used this way of thinking. He was really upset about the way his flesh kept leading him into thinking, saying and doing things that he bitterly regretted but he would say, "It's not me, it's not 'I'"

There are things about us that we take for granted and never examine. We take it as read that these things are part of who we are. These things seem to have us, we do not have them; they hold us, we do not hold them. If I *have* an apple there are a number of things I can do with it: throw it, eat it, stew it. If I *am* an apple I can only hang there from the tree and wait to be acted upon. The world of *being* an apple, is a world filled with things we never question or doubt and is a world of powerlessness. The world in which we *have* the apple, by contrast, is the world where transformations can occur and new perspectives can be gained. It is pregnant with possibilities.

We are not the horses. We are the driver, but we have got so used to uncontrolled emotions and appetites getting their way that it feels as though we have lost any real sense of being the driver at all. It feels as though we have become the horses; that we have become the "flesh." But if I take that one simple step of saying to myself: "This is not me," I can start to at least begin to imagine that I can truly be the driver again. I was in control once so therefore I *could* be in control again.

So the first step on the road to lasting transformation is to take up a position outside of ourselves, outside of the thinking we never question or doubt which leads to the habits we so deeply regret.[1] What I am up against is not myself but something that is parasitic upon my self. And I can take responsibility for it because I am not it. It is powerful, this thing, yet not as powerful as me. My "I," my self, after all, is fully personal. The behavior that is parasitic upon me, by contrast, is a mere "it." It is only a vicious cycle of negative thoughts trying to be resolved. It is only a certain set of feelings that keep being triggered by the same old things. As we shall explore, it has personal, rather beastly, qualities; it even has a voice, but it is not fully personal, and is therefore inferior and possible to defeat.

---

1. This idea of standing outside of ourselves is what Ben has tried to illustrate in the slightly weird picture at the start of this chapter. It is a collage he made out of two drawings he did of the same guy.

Pause for Thought: Is there a difference between saying, "I am an awful person," and "I have done some awful things"?

Some More Pictures

Some, rather than using this word "flesh," or going on about horses and apples, have found the word "illness" or "disease" helpful. Daniel found it helpful to see his addiction to party drugs as an illness. This helped him to separate his healthy "me" from the sick "me."

Jack Trimpey uses the idea of a voice. He helps us to see that addictions can have a life of their own: it is as though they are talking back to us whenever we try to kick the habit. He calls this the Addictive Voice, the AV:

> When you recognize and understand your AV, it becomes not-you, but 'it,' an easily defeated enemy that has been causing you to drink. . .Complete separation of 'you' from 'it' leads to complete recovery and hope for a better life.[2]

So, it seems that this ability to take a step back from our addiction is a good deal of the battle won. Indeed, Trimpey, an experienced recovery expert and former alcoholic, seems convinced that this recognition alone of the otherness of the "Beast"[3] is the main key to recovery. This beast knows only one answer to everything. An alcoholic Beast, for instance, would suggest only one thing in response to the need to celebrate, relax, mourn, overcome depression, deal with tiredness, loss, anxiety, resentment, or despair: "Have a drink." Devious and subtle it can be; creative or original it never is! But being fully human gives us a tremendous advantage.[4]

2. Trimpey, *Rational Recovery*, 34.

3. He has even made the term "Beast," as well as "Addictive Voice Recognition Technique," "AVRT," "RR," "Addiction Diction" and "Big Plan" into proprietary service marks (the equivalent of Trade Marks) for his Rational Recovery Systems, Inc. Such altruistic chaps these recovery therapists!

4. Trimpey, *Rational Recovery*, 36.

In C.S. Lewis' fantasy about heaven, *The Great Divorce*,[5] a man is described who has a little red lizard which lives on his shoulder. The lizard is constantly whispering bad things into his ear. An angel offers to kill it but must gain the man's permission first since he cannot override his free will. The man has doubts. He likes his lizard; he cannot imagine life without it. And the lizard, desperate for its own survival, also makes its case, telling the man that he cannot really live without him. Repeatedly the angel has to reassure the man that, though it will hurt to remove the troublesome and embarrassing little lizard, it will not kill the man. The angel repeats his question again and again: "May I kill it?" and, "Have I your permission?" Eventually, permission is given and the angel grabs the writhing lizard and hurls it to the ground. After an initial cry of pain, the man grows from a faint shadowy figure into someone magnificent.

During the early days of his recovery, Daniel would see himself as two people; one entirely addicted, requiring constant indulgence, and seeking to manipulate his better self and everyone else into getting what it wants. It always seemed to have a plan to lure him into agreeing with it. It would make him feel sad or guilty, or perhaps resentful or jealous of others. The one goal of Addict Daniel was to go back to drug addiction and if it couldn't do that, it would settle for using computer games or social media addictively. It did not care about people, or for himself, and it would never, of course, honor Daniel's request for it to leave. But Daniel also had an entirely recovered self. He was quieter. He did not need to be indulged, or to shout to remain content. In fact, he was so content in himself that he could stare blankly at a wall and be entirely satisfied. Unlike the Addict Daniel, Recovered Daniel was constructive; he was always looking for the betterment of himself and others, and seeking to find a way to make himself the most useful version of

5. Lewis, *The Great Divorce*, 106–112. Ben is indebted to Cliff College graduate John Bell for highlighting this part of C.S. Lewis' work.

himself. He always looked for the positive in any situation, and recognized the good in everyone, including himself. Perhaps most crucially, Recovered Daniel was and is far greater than Addict Daniel. Addict Daniel is primal and basic; Recovered Daniel is developed and complicated. Clearly, given the choice between the two, it is clear which person Daniel would strive to be. But if he had not actively chosen recovery, he would have chosen addiction by default because of the controlling tactics of Addict Daniel.

So, we have thought about chariot horses and apples, lizards on the shoulder and voices that perpetuate the addiction, and we have talked about diseases. In all these ways we have been saying that you always have a choice: not between a number of different things—it's not even that complicated—but just a choice, at every turn and in the face of every temptation, between just two options. To pick up on Trimpey's voice idea, there are always two voices. There is a voice that says "I must have this and have it right now. I cannot stand being denied this," or "I feel upset so I must drink this, must take this to calm me, soothe me: it's what I do." And there is a quieter voice, one that is reasonable, peaceable, rational. It is not excessive, demanding, strict, or condemning. If you listen out you will find that this other more reasonable voice is *always* there, however faintly. The key difference is in the tone: the one is demanding, has no morals and misses out important facts such as the short term pleasure and long term harm of the action; the other voice is gentle, kind and honest. Even to recognize that there are these two voices, and to no longer keep trying to make the unreasonable voice seem reasonable, is probably at least half the battle won. A former porn addict put it this way, ". . . there are two dogs in my heart's backyard. One dog always craves pleasure, sin and selfishness. The other dog craves justice, mercy, peace and obedience to God. When I wake up every day, I choose which dog gets fed. The one I feed grows until the other dog can't even be seen."[6]

No one is claiming that this is easy. We have obeyed the wrong impulse for so long it has steadily grown in power, which is what we will look at in Step 2.

Questions:

1. Have you ever thought of your bad behavior as an "it" or do you normally think of it as part of who you are?

2. In what ways does it help you to think of your dark side as not you?

Further Reading:

Romans 7:7–25; Galatians 5:16–25

Jack Trimpey, *Rational Recovery: The New Cure for Substance Addiction* (New York: Pocket Books, 1996).

6. Groves, "I'm a Christian Addicted to Porn." *Christianity Today.* [accessed online 1 Nov 2016] http://www.christianitytoday.com/iyf/truelifestories/ithappenedtome/im-christian-addicted-to-porn.html?start=2

2

TAKE STOCK

'Better luck next time!' the dealer shouted, trying to cheer me up. I quickly turned so he wouldn't see the tears streaming down my face. I was thirty thousand dollars in debt, my twenty-year marriage was nearly destroyed, and my four children no longer trusted me. I'd hit rock bottom.

> The casino's neon lights shined brightly in the midnight sky as I left to get into my car. I turned back for one final look at a building that represented what had become my obsession during the past three years. I finally realized what I'd become—a compulsive gambler.[1]

Our passions and appetites can be an awesome foe. The ancients used to refer to this part of our lives as something like an evil ruler or monster. One of the ancient philosophers described just how bad it can get:

> I am overcome by evil, and I realise what evil I am about to do, but my passion controls my plans.[2]

The 2004 movie, *Without a Paddle* is a comedy that charts the adventures of three men on a quest through the mountain forests of Oregon. At one point they find themselves hopelessly cornered by an angry grizzly bear. It raises itself on its hind legs, lifts its paws in readiness for a good mauling, and lets out a terrifying raw. The smallest (and most anxious) of the three men does not make it to the tree where the other two men have begun climbing to safety. One of the men (Dax Shepard) then remembers that he had read somewhere that, in such situations, the best thing to do is to get into the fetal position, then the bear will leave you alone. The small man (Matthew Lillard), still terrified, tries out this advice and curls himself into a tiny ball on the ground, closes his eyes and whimpers pathetically as the huge bear towers over him. The advice works. In fact it works too well: the bear starts to think he is a cub and picks him up by his clothes with its teeth and starts trying to feed him some raw meat. The small man pretends so well that he is enjoying the food that the bear goes off to get some more, which proves to be the man's only chance of escape.

The Apostle Paul used to describe our big hairy bear as the "flesh," a word we met in the previous chapter. It is a power that rules (Romans 6:12), enslaves (Romans 6:13, 18, 20; 7:14), makes

---

1. Chambers, "What I Lost By Gambling."

2. Euripidies, *Medaea* lines 1078–9. Translation offered by Royce, "Early Stoicism and Akrasia," 315.

war (Romans 7:23), imprisons (Romans 7:23) and even kills us (Romans 7:10, 11, 13)!

Thinking back to the chariot driver idea: normally, we can at least trust the driver. That is, we can normally trust ourselves and keep ourselves in the driver's seat, despite the fact that we might be having a little bother with our highly spirited horses. But there are times when even our rational selves can get so accustomed to bad actions having the last word that it begins to follow willingly. Emotions and pleasures can run rampant for so long that the core you has become corrupt. You have become part of the problem. The tail is now wagging the dog. We are in a state in which, every day, we stare despairingly in the face of that deepest of human mysteries: why we keep acting *against* our better judgment. It feels like a situation in which the chariot driver has jumped off the chariot and is now riding on one of the horses and having a thoroughly wild time. The situation seems *completely* out of control.

I would contend, though, that there is still a core you that hates what you do. In fact, it is that very hatred that lets you know you're still in there somewhere. There's your evidence. You're still there so there's hope.

Pause for Thought: What have been the times when you have felt the most hopeless about your addiction? You are here today so something must have given you hope again. What was it?

Victory from the Teeth of Defeat

What often happens once we rediscover a glimmer of something of us that would like to overcome the habit is that we try and fight using our will power. We might even succeed for a while. But we have forgotten how dysfunctional even the most rational part of us has become, how corrupted we are, how incapable of changing anything in our own strength. What happens is that the initial success produces pride and we start to assume we can handle it. We become over confident, forgetting the sheer madness we were in for so long. We might start to find that we can only remember the fun moments in our addiction and quickly forget all the misery, waste and ruin.

This deluded state of mind leads quite soon to a relapse and a feeling of even greater powerlessness. It is then that we realize this thing is bigger than we are. Sure, we can still say, as we did at Step 1, that it's not us but we have given it so much power that it is now bigger than us and we are so corrupted it has become more powerful than us. It has become like a huge grizzly bear towering over us. But the real breakthrough comes when we accept this and stop trying to compete with that which is so obviously bigger than we are. In fact, the best thing seems to be the exact opposite position to fighting: one of abject humility. We curl ourselves into a ball on the ground, helpless. This is counter-intuitive because the last thing humans tend to do when faced with a monstrously dominant power is bow low before it.[3]

Known as "Bill W" because of AA's commitment to keeping everyone anonymous, William Griffith Wilson (1895–1971) came from a broken home ending up deserted by both parents and tried to mask his pain through an all-out pursuit of success as a New York stock broker. His first experiences of drinking at parties were of a dramatic easing of his awkward social shyness. He suddenly felt at ease with himself and others.

Over time, Wilson's activities in business became more and more hampered by his drinking until finally, in 1933, his alcoholism had got so bad he was admitted to hospital. There his friend Ebby Thatcher visited him and told him straight: "Realize you are licked, admit it, and get willing to turn your life over to the care of God."[4] In 1934, while in hospital for the fourth time, a crucial event took place:

3. Buker, "Spiritual Development and the Epistemology of Systems Theory," 143–153.

4. Tim Stafford, "The Hidden Gospel of the 12 Steps," *Christianity Today*

My depression deepened unbearably and finally it seemed to me as though I were at the very bottom of the pit. I still gagged badly on the notion of a Power greater than myself, but finally, just for the moment, the last vestige of my proud obstinacy was crushed. All at once I found myself crying out, 'If there is a God, let Him show Himself! I am ready to do anything, anything.'

Suddenly the room lit up with a great white light. I was caught up into an ecstasy which there are no words to describe. It seemed to me, in a mind's eye, that I was on a mountain and that a wind not of air but of spirit was blowing. Slowly the ecstasy subsided. I lay on the bed, but for a time I was in another world, a new world of consciousness. All about me and through me was a wonderful feeling of Presence, and I thought to myself, 'So this is the God of the preachers!

Alcoholics Anonymous speak about "turning it over." AA participants understand that the issues are all about power. We tend to quite stubbornly insist that we have the power to master a problem that has got out of control. To admit that we cannot control ourselves is frightening but necessary. Bill Wilson knew that only a power higher than him, a power that wasn't him, could rescue him. Here he is again: "The more we become willing to depend on a Higher Power, the more independent we actually are. Therefore dependence, as AA practices it, is really a means of gaining true independence of the spirit."[5]

But to get this power, we have to be willing to completely turn over our lives. Having one foot in recovery and one foot in addiction is a very troubling place. Daniel has observed that many people linger on the brink of this decision for a long of time. But change this great will not happen unless you allow it. Remember the question of the angel in the *Great Divorce*: "Have I your permission?"

(July 22 1991), p. 14.

5. Wilson, *Alcoholics Anonymous*, 36.

Jason escaped into addiction to cover his feelings of fear and inadequacy, but this was just the start. Addiction soon ruled his every thought and action. He describes how he celebrated and mourned using drink and drugs. He was soon using brandy to come off heroin taking him deeper into a whole complex of addictions and poor coping techniques. His life was full of illness and despair. It was the law of diminishing returns. His bodily organs began to break down and his body started rejecting food.

Loneliness ruled, he says. He recalls spending three weeks in hospital and being told that he had only months to live, yet even this sobering fact was not enough. He had not a single visitor and on leaving hospital he picked up a drink, thinking, "This is it: my end is coming and I will soon be leaving this world, I may as well go drunk."

Well, he didn't die. In fact, life carried on in this state for a further three years, including some periods of homelessness, before being again admitted into hospital, and then into the care of the Salvation Army. For the first time in his life he was forced to go without. He managed only three weeks in a rehab before relapsing over one very boozy weekend with his brother. He admitted this on his return to the Rehab and was asked to leave, but there was a group that met on the Wednesday, which was part of another organization. He remembers thinking, when he got there: "I've got nothing and nowhere to go," so he gave his whole story at the group, holding nothing back, which was promptly greeted with a round of applause and an offer to stay residentially with the project and continue his recovery.

He was encouraged to seek a peer mentor to help him to engage with the AA process. At the group he met a man who became his sponsor, and, since then, became a lifelong friend. Jason was told to find a "higher power," a god of his own understanding. This was not difficult as he was volunteering at a Christian charity shop and he could ask the workers to teach him more about God. He went along to church and met other

Christians. He enjoyed singing the upbeat songs in the service and soon took part in an "Alpha" course to learn more about the Christian faith.

So far, so good. Jason was in what he describes as "early recovery," but all was not well yet. For a start, he was having nightmares every night. He spoke to his sponsor at AA about it, and his response was unforgettably simple, but life changing. He simply told Jason to "pray," which was not something he had been given to doing until then. That night he asked God to lift the nightmares and help him to sleep. Jason was amazed to wake up the following morning completely refreshed having not had any bad dreams. This got Jason thinking: "If he could do that, maybe he could lift my addiction." He prayed that very thing and, from that day until this, he has not drunk a drop of alcohol or taken an illicit drug.

Profit and Loss

We have countless stories of people discovering God in the midst of the chaos of addiction. This was Daniel's experience. And now he says that the main reason he does not take drugs is that he has found something so much better. The life he enjoys with God far outweighs the life he had with drugs. He knows that he could not have recovered without God but adds that he does not know why he would have even wanted to recover without Him. He recalls hearing a man in an AA meeting say that by giving his life over to God, it felt like he never quit anything. Quitting sounded like loss, but he had not lost anything. Instead, the comfort he found in drink he found in God, and permanently. Better yet, he had to do nothing detestable to sustain it.

Dealing with the flesh involves losing power to gain power; relinquishing self-effort in order to gain true control. Are you ready to admit defeat yet? Are you ready to embrace the pain of self-humbling to experience the abundant life of Christ living in you and through you? To use the language of AA, are you ready to step out of the driving seat? Are you ready to "let go and let God"?

Tony came to a Priory recovery group for the first time "drunk as a skunk," and riding his motorbike. His wife had said to him that if he didn't get well she would leave him. This ultimatum brought him to the point of wanting to engage with the first three steps of the 12-Step system. These first three steps meant that he admitted that he had become powerless over his drinking but then also came to believe that a power greater than himself could restore him and then turned his life over to the care of God. This was not a one-off event for Tony, however. It was a gradual process of coming to a deeper and deeper realization of these three things. In the end, Tony's recovery was so attractive to Jason that he became Jason's biggest inspiration on his own path to recovery.

Honesty: Your Secret Weapon

One of the biggest obstacles to gambling addicts being able to recover is the fact that lying, both to others and to themselves, is even more a part of the addictive behavior with this type of addiction than it is with other types. But this highlights something that is true of all addictions. "Problem gamblers usually do not have to think about lying and deception," says gambling addiction expert Michael Vlach, "it comes naturally."[6] One former gambling addict sadly recollects: "I was beginning to lie to my own parents. Even to my own husband. I was beginning to believe my own lies; that's the saddest thing."[7]

6. Vlach, *Chance to Change*, cited in Vlach, "Escaping the Lies of Gambling Addiction." *Christianity* [accessed online 1 Nov 2016] http://www.christianity.com/1289790/

7. Ibid.

We must look at ourselves with the most brutal honesty. If we don't then life will do it for us sooner or later, and it will not be a pleasant experience. We do not need to hit bottom to get the breakthrough, we just need to be honest with ourselves and those closest to us, we just need to humble ourselves and relinquish our control.

So What Are You Waiting For?

This core idea of losing power to gain power, so much at the heart of 12-Step recovery, should not surprise us. Jesus spoke in this way all the time, saying that the rich must become small enough to fit through the eye of a needle, and that all of us need to contract ourselves to the size of little children: humble, unassuming and dependent. He even talked about losing your life in order to find it. He kept on confronting the human assumption that we can do it for ourselves. Paul the Apostle, likewise, came to realize that trying to make himself good only made him even more rebellious. In other words, it is a process that all of us need to go through, even those who would not claim to be addicted to anything.

Psalm 34 is a great Psalm to use. In that Psalm, David keeps referring to himself, as well as all passionate seekers after God, as the "the humble" (verse 2) the "poor man" (verse 6), the "broken" (verse 18), and "his servants" (verse 22). If you can describe yourself as one of these then the Psalm promises that you will be glad (verse 2), the Lord will answer you (verse 4) and deliver you from all your troubles (verse 6), and this Lord is already near to you (verse 18) and will not condemn you (verse 22).

Action: If you believe in God, kneel or bow before him and admit that you cannot handle this on your own and call out for help. Let him know you really mean it.

Further reading:

Psalm 34

Bill Wilson, *Alcoholics Anonymous: The Story of How Many Thousands of Men and Women Have Recovered from Alcoholism* (New York: Alcoholics Anonymous World Services, New York, 1995)

3

ACQUIRE A NEW MASTER

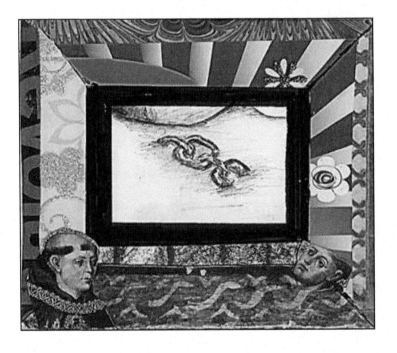

The Power of a Firm Resolve

Alice became an alcoholic over the six years of her father's long illness. He had cancer, for which he refused treatment and his suffering and eventual death was a source of great pain to Alice. In the wake of his death, she nearly drank herself to death and her alcoholism led to her children being taken into care. Being determined to get her children back, she went for treatment to get completely dry. For Alice maintaining abstinence was to do with stubbornness. Jason says that she won't drink because she's "so damn stubborn." Faith has played a part in this and she now attends a lively church. Today she never even thinks about having a drink, but if it were not for her tenacity at the start, this state of not even wanting to drink could not have been reached.

Recovery is like a spring: the harder you push into it, the further it will propel you into a new life.

Ian was a man who, while grieving over the loss of both parents, started drinking heavily and smoking marijuana. In time, he was drinking beer and vodka and smoking weed all day every day. But he got to the point where he was sick and tired of being tired and sick. His drinking was so bad that when he came to see Jason, he had to be given a drink just to stop his body from going into shock. He was drinking around 500 units per week, but his plan was simple: to cut down his drinking by half a can a day. Never once did he deviate from the plan. In fact, it worked so well that, once he was completely dry, he used a similar schedule for cutting down on weed by a spliff a day, making the allocated number of spliffs each morning and reducing these from ten to zero.

In contrast to our characters Alice and Ian above, some people who attempt recovery never commit to truly changing. Naturally, we are going to be conflicted. It is difficult to give up the thing that brings us the most comfort and go whole heartedly into the unknown. Many of us test the waters of recovery but never actually *choose* to recover. *Choosing* to recover means choosing to allow the addiction to die, and that is very scary.

Vince had inherited a six bedroom house in Jamaica which he looked forward to using for holidays and eventual retirement. His childhood in Jamaica had been centered on the church and his mother was a devout Christian. However, in the UK he was mixing with all the wrong people and became involved in crack-cocaine, first as a dealer, rising to become the top dealer in the city, and then as a raging addict. Vince was arrested for the importation and supply of drugs. When in prison, and at the end of himself, he resolved he would learn his lesson. This pain was not to be wasted. He decided, "I have done prison once and once only. This is not going to happen again." It was a clean decision. When he got out, he had to change his circle of friends and move out of the area and began helping out on a faith-based recovery program teaching others the secrets of recovery. He never touched drugs again. Today, Jason speaks of him as a man who is full of faith and full of love for others.

We sympathize with anyone in a situation where a hard choice must be made. There is comfort in addiction. If there wasn't, our behavior would have changed by itself. Our addictive activity has become so ingrained that, when we do finally choose recovery, it feels like accepting death. In fact, choosing recovery is a kind of a death. Daniel could not envision a life without drugs. He believed he would never be happy, never have friends, never go out, never feel alright without a substance in his body. The only memories he had of not using were the times during addiction when he was waiting for drugs, and he certainly did not want to experience that for the rest of his life! After all, he was only eighteen. His recovered life would be long!

The Secret of Recovering Well

So, what exactly does choosing recovery look like? It is now that we come close to the heart of the problem and its solution. And really, the best way to explain it is by using this word "love." What we love describes what we serve, and what we serve describes what has the most say in our lives, what has the most power. But love can only work by way of desire. Our strongest desires are to serve whatever it is that we truly love. For too long our deepest desire has been to serve a master called "addiction." It is as though we are in love with it. We can think about little else.

For this reason, the single most crucial step we can take is to do something about our desires. We have to subjugate them, subordinate them, put them in their rightful place. We have to make them serve a new master. And we do this, not because we are damaging our health or reputation, and not because we feel bad and want to live a happier life, or because we are threatened by divorce or prison. As we saw with Jason in hospital being told he did not have long to live, these scares may bring sorrow and remorse but will not necessarily bring a lasting breakthrough.

The truth is this: only *love* can make us *hate* our bad behavior enough to give it up. Often, a human relationship will give us sufficient motivation. Some people that have lived a fairly wild kind of life can change a lot when they meet someone and fall in love. For the sake of that relationship, they will give up their old lifestyle. One former sex addict put it this way: "It isn't easy but when you love someone you do change, I have always been able to do things for other people that I cannot do for myself."[1]

But what about those cases we hear of—and we might be guilty of this ourselves—where a pattern of behavior has become so ingrained that we frankly no longer care who we hurt? In those cases there needs to be a kind of love that exceeds any other. This kind of love is so strong that all will fall before it. It is love for our

---

1. Fantelli, citing "Becky" in, "Sex, Sex, Sex': The Story of a Female Sex Addict." *Mental Healthy.* Accessed Online 1 Nov 2016: http://www.mentalhealthy. co.uk/news/924-female-sex-addiction.html

flawless and loving Creator. It is a love we were born to have and fills us with the highest satisfaction and joy. To express that love to him is to place ourselves entirely beyond the reach of our big fat hairy bear, our beast. It is a signal to him that we have changed masters and are no longer in his service.

So why is love so important? Because, in the end, it will cause us to simply grow out of our biggest problems. It is frankly the easiest and best solution possible.

Pause for Thought: Think back to a time before you were addicted. What did you love then? Was there something you enjoyed that was good but which you have now lost?

We can explore this idea of loving something or someone more than your addiction a bit further. Robert Kegan is a thinker who has come up with a theory about how humans develop which he calls the 'evolving self.'[2] His framework is as follows:

First Order Consciousness

This is the stage of infancy in which babies and young toddlers are beginning to process and manipulate the world around them via the senses. They are also beginning to identify themselves as distinct from others and with their own unique needs and they are able to start articulating those needs. Almost all adults have got past this stage.

Second Order Consciousness

This is the phase of late childhood. At this point, children begin to be conscious of fixed needs and likes and dislikes and can articulate these proficiently. They are also only just beginning to realize that the expectations of others, the rules of good behavior, are going to

2. Kegan, *The Evolving Self*. A development on these theories is his *In Over Our Heads: The Mental Demands of Modern Life*.

be the same tomorrow as they were today. This is why, until about the age of seven, there is a tendency to apparently keep forgetting the rules and the consequences of breaking them.

Through discipline and negotiation with friends and siblings they learn that their needs have to be balanced with other people's needs, though they are not yet able to fully grasp the importance of that and struggle to genuinely subordinate their needs for the sake of their relationships with others.

There are many adults that are stuck at this stage who do not necessarily have a disability. They are what would be described as 'sociopaths.' Psychologists would say they have a personality disorder. They are tyrannically selfish and repeatedly fail to genuinely understand the importance of other people's needs. Subordinating their own needs to the needs of a relationship—in other words, socialization—never truly happens. They have never moved beyond seeing others as a means to an end. They compensate for this with the use of charm or bullying. They feel different to everyone else—inferior—and never feel at ease with themselves. They are prone to addictions, especially to alcohol, and often end up in prison. They are narcissistic and can be ruthlessly ambitious in a quest for self-aggrandizement.

Third Order of Consciousness

This is the stage that is reached at some point during teen-hood. At this age, parents hope that their children will begin to internalize moral norms to the point where they will come home on time not because of threats but because they value their relationship with their parents. At this age, adolescents learn to subordinate their short term needs to the longer term needs of a relationship. Most people come out the other end of those years having become fully socialized. In fact, early adulthood tends to be the most sociable phase in a person's life when many lifelong friends are made and marriage partners are often identified. It is during this third order of consciousness that love for others starts to bring about this illusive thing called maturity. It is love that makes us behave like adults. It is love that makes us self-forgetful and self-giving. And it is want of it that makes us unable to break out of cycles of self-centered behavior.

Daniel had next to no compassion for anyone until he met Christ. Before that, every action was self-serving. He would generally only help anyone if it served his interests in some way. This was true even of his close family, even of those he ought to have loved the most. He would often help his mother in a seemingly selfless way but his goal was to use his helpfulness for personal gain later. He would purposely rekindle the affections she had for him as a child by hugging her, or spending quality time with her. He even believed that he was doing right by her. The reality, as Daniel now freely admits, is that he lied constantly, stole off her daily and used her as leverage over the rest of his family. Similar behavior showed itself in every other relationship he had. He was cruelly manipulative. Then, while in treatment for his addiction, he wrestled with the concept of having love for others. He remembers speaking to counselors about the lack of love he felt for anyone and was given some great advice—wisdom that will work for anyone seeking recovery: change your behavior and your thinking will follow. It is through the action we take that we see change, not through our thoughts or intentions. We become the people we actively strive to be. In Daniel's case, he had to change his manipulative nature. Practicing love, after all, is easy if there is a pay-out at the end. So, instead, he tried to help people when they were not aware. At church, he cleaned toilets and did things that most people had no idea he had done. He began to love it. Naturally, trying to help people causes you to think a lot more about them: what their likes and dislikes are, what they want and what they need. Daniel's thoughts did indeed change as a result of a change in his behavior.

It may be arduous at first, but ultimately, a changed way of thinking is what every addict in recovery should be seeking. It is not enough to cut the behavior out, but still obsess over it, wishing it was part of your life. True recovery involves a psychological change, where indulging in addictive behavior has no appeal at all. You have grown out of it.

Pause for Thought: Who are you deep down inside? Are you a child only thinking of others as ways of supplying what you need? Are you a teenager trying to put others first but often failing when negative feelings take over? Are you an adult but with an addiction that is making you act more and more selfishly?

The Greatest Love of All

There is no power like the power of deciding to love God. Paul found this to be true. He had been addicted to his Jewish identity. He had trusted in his own status as a fine upstanding religionist: a leading light in the community, and with an impeccable pedigree. But then he crashed. He describes having gone through a kind of a death, saying, "I through the law died to the law" (Galatians 2:19). The Jewish laws that he had once kept had caused him to die. The very zeal with which he had kept them had led him nowhere good. In fact, in his misguided radicalism, he had even ended up becoming a violent and hateful man. But then, he met Christ who came to him like a blinding light and knocked him off his horse one day on the road to Damascus. From that time, the old bigotry had become like death to him and Christ had become everything to him: "What things were gain to me, these I have counted loss for Christ. Indeed, I count all things loss for the excellence of the knowledge of Christ Jesus my Lord, for whom I have lost all things and count them as rubbish [literally "excrement"] that I may gain Christ. . ." (Philippians 3:7–8)

Love for God is the love we were born to have. It is the most natural thing in the world to feel it. When this love comes to town it fills us with the highest satisfaction and joy. To simply say with Paul: "I count everything as loss if only I may have you, God," is to turn your back on your old master. Even so, we are not expected to spontaneously produce a wholehearted devotion to God that instantly transforms our lives. Generations of mystics discovered, however, that by constant meditation on Christ and all he has done for us, their emotions were touched and their wills were moved so that they could more easily keep their minds off themselves. Take St Anselm, for instance. He even talked to himself about this love he had for the Saviour who died for him: "think of what you owe your Saviour. Consider what he was to you, what he did for you, and think that for what he did for you he is the more worthy to be loved."[3] St Bernard was convinced that: "Of all the sentiments and affections, love is the only one that allows the creature to respond to the Creator. . ."[4] It is a love that moves us to change our ways.

Action: List some ways in which some specific loving actions could help you to put someone's needs above your own.

Action: If you have faith in Christ, kneel before him and let him know that, because he gave up everything for you, he is worth everything to you. Even if you have known Christ for years, now may be the time to bow low before him and let him know again that he is Lord. If it helps, say these words: *What things were gain to me these I now count as loss for You, the one who loved me and gave himself up for me. I now turn my whole life over to You and receive Your Spirit into my heart to help me live for You.* Do this as often as it takes.

Further Reading:

Philippians 3:7–8

Robert Kegan, *The Evolving Self* (Cambridge, MA: Harvard University Press, 1982).

3. Ward (Ed), *The Prayers and Meditations of St Anselm*, 235.
4. Bernard, *Sermons on the Song of Songs* 83:4.

4

MAKE A DEEP CONNECTION

The Hidden Wonders of the Deep Mind

So we are beginning to love enough to hate what we do enough to stop. But, as we saw, this thing is bigger than we are. It would be foolish to underestimate its power. It is true that it is a product of our passions and appetites and only has the power that we have given to it. We gave it this power. Trouble is, over the years, we have given it such a lot of power it has acquired a life of its own. Be assured, though, that there will always be a core you that genuinely wants to change and not just to play the recovery game or the therapy game or the New Year's resolutions game. Inside this core you and core me is a deep well of invaluable inner resources which no one can take from us, and which we desperately need to draw from if we are to water our parched lives.

This inner well has recently been termed the 'deep mind.' This deep mind is entirely different to the other mind, which has been called the 'self-conscious mind.' This idea of two minds within us is closely related to the older ideas of an unconscious and a conscious mind, and very closely tied to the idea of the intuitive right brain and the logical left brain. The right-hand side of our brains is where we have deep wordless thoughts that are really creative and resourceful. Breakthroughs happen here. Discoveries and eureka moments erupt from this area of thought. Tapping into it opens to us fresh reserves of energy and inner peace, like unblocking a long disused well or spring of fresh clear water.

The other mind, the self-conscious or analytical mind, which is in the left-hand side of our brains, is also needed. Without this way of thinking we would not be able to organize and articulate the deep but wordless truths the deep mind of the right side of our brains gives us. It is this side of our thinking that tends to be more focused. But there is a downside to this. In addictions that power to focus on things is what makes us really obsessive about our next fix. We are literally fixated. So this way of thinking needs to be suspended if we are to get a proper drink from the well of the deep mind. The kind of thinking that happens in the left side of our brains is always looking at itself, turned in on itself, locked into various loops and cycles of thinking, many of which are behind our worst habits. And it is always trying to figure things out, always analyzing and evaluating everything and everybody, oh, and it loves to think it is in control and that it always has a perfect grasp of everything. The truth is that because it is always verbally constructing truth and creating systems, it is prone to distorting things in the process. Things get out of shape as it tries to make everything fit together properly. It does not have the power to gain a complete vision of everything. Big insights into the real nature of things belong to the vast wordless space of the deep mind. It is also there that we meet the Creator in a major way and this will prove crucial.

Jason compares this shift to experiencing God in recovery as like changing from an old car that had only manual steering to a newer one with powered steering. Ben owns two cars: one is an old Peugeot with manual gears, manual steering, manual everything. Just getting anywhere in it is like a work-out. His other car is a one year old Renault Zoe: all electric with a virtually silent engine. It glides everywhere effortlessly, has automatic transmission, an on-board computer and a steering wheel that is smooth as butter. The Apostle Paul used to say to his young congregations: "Walk in the Spirit and you will not gratify the desires of the flesh" (Galatians 5:16). It really can be that easy. In our own strength, no, but in the Spirit there is a power that is not our own and which takes the hard work out of everything.

But where do we start with deepening our connection to God's almighty power?

Purging

All the mystics insisted on this and some described a very lengthy purifying process. The reality is, I think, rather more prosaic and a lot less demanding. It is a simple practical fact that, when you meditate, whatever is going on in you will be intensified, which is why meditation can be dangerous. If you meditate while you are feeling angry, for instance, the anger will intensify. To help clear the ground you might try writing down the rage, or the shame, or the lust that you feel, then destroying the paper.

Meditating

The commonest form of meditation is one-pointed meditation. It is like throwing a ball to a dog. Your self-conscious mind is the dog and it needs to busy itself focusing on something. You send it off by getting it to focus on one point: maybe a single word, or perhaps by counting your breaths as they leave your nose: starting at ten and finishing at one, then starting again. Christians have traditionally meditated on Scripture, perhaps a single phrase or a scene from a Bible story, or sometimes the phrase "Lord, Jesus, Christ, Son, of God, have, mercy, on, me," with a breath for every word. One biblical phrase which works well is "Be Still (focus on stilling yourself) . . . and know (allow that part of you that is deeper than words, deeper than thought itself, to connect with God) . . . that I (choose one member of the Trinity: Father, Son or Holy Spirit) . . . am God (allow that member of the Trinity to be God to you in ways that meet your deepest need)." Or, you may prefer to focus on each body part, attending to each part to ensure it is completely relaxed. One nun once described how she focused on the body and on spiritual things in a kind of progression: "I silence my body to listen to my mind. I silence my mind to listen to my heart. I silence my heart to listen to my spirit. I silence my spirit to listen to God."

The other type of meditation, now emulated in Mindfulness, is open monitoring. In open monitoring we allow thoughts to come and go—one answer to porn addiction, for instance, is called "urge surfing," in which you allow a sexual urge to appear but then imagine yourself riding it to shore and letting it break harmlessly on the beach. And we let ourselves be aware of what is going on around us; we often keep our eyes open. Mantras that can help with this style of meditation include these: "O my God, You are here; O my God, I am here; O my God, we are here, and always, always, You love us," or, "I dwell in the present moment (breathing in); it is the most wonderful moment (breathing out)." It is crucially important to train your mind to be in the moment. Addictive thoughts always take us away somewhere else. Addictive urges are always trying to make us want to be somewhere else doing something else instead of being content. Open monitoring allows you to appreciate the beauty around you and enjoy the little sounds that humanity and nature make all the time.

Beholding

The deep mind is where you get your brightest ideas and is where God speaks, but you only get to see the contents of it by looking at it out of the corner of your eye, so to speak. You get there by not trying to get there. And you do not necessarily fall into a trance: it is possible to carry on doing things such as gardening at the same time. Some novelists routinely tune into this side of them in order to be creative at the start of each writing session. Roald Dahl, one of the most imaginative children's writers of modern times, would sit in a particular arm chair, lower his chin to his chest and enter a deep thinking state before writing. Poetry, music and art are generated and appreciated via this part of us so it is not completely unfamiliar territory, but learning to engage deeply with it and encounter God through it might well be.

Engaging with your deep mind, listening to your heart, might initially seem wholly unspectacular, but the effect it will have on the rest of your day could be dramatic. We have certainly found it so. You will find that the allurements of the world no longer interest you and that cravings weaken. Your thought life will come alive with insights. You will have a sense of direction, vision and purpose that seems clearer. Because you are now more deeply rooted in who you really are, you will find that you are more secure and less defensive. You might also find that, in prayer, you ask for fewer and simpler things and that praying for other people instead of yourself comes more naturally.

Of all the Twelve Steps, Step Eleven fast became Daniel's favorite; "[we] sought through prayer and meditation to improve our conscious contact with God as we understood him. . ." Meditating and praying was a luxury Daniel could not afford while he was caught in addiction. His brain was always switched on. He was permanently wired. He could not sleep or concentrate on a menial task without feeling total frustration. It was maddening. The ability to sit, finally free, is one of the gems of recovery for Daniel. He suggests that if you struggle to truly connect with God, try to strip away the things you think you know about God, and instead ask Him to make Himself known to you.

Pause for Thought: Think back to when you last got a bright idea. That was your deep well talking to you. What was it that helped? What were you doing or not doing at the time that helped this fresh thinking to flourish?

Connecting with other People

The Blessings

Recovery is not only about connecting with God, however. The quality of your connectedness to people will be a key indicator of how well you recover. Remember Rat Park?

It is common for our addictions to isolate us. A lot of addiction is the product of avoiding all of the potential pain that comes from our interactions with people. Early recovery is particularly difficult in this respect. It is so much easier to hide away than to face the world and the people in it. But loneliness is toxic. Loneliness makes us much more likely to try and fix our feelings by returning to our addiction.

Churches can be a great place to start connecting again with others. A good church will make an effort to talk to new people and make them feel at home. Many have house groups and social activities that run throughout the year which allow for healthy human interaction. Addiction groups, church-based and non-church based, are also probably functioning in your neighborhood.

Will was a man who needed a group setting because he needed direction. He was referred to Jason at a point in his life when he had just set fire to his apartment. He had lived a chaotic life of drink and drugs and prostitutes. He arrived at rehab with a huge unkempt beard, and swearing and cursing. He was so out of control he needed to be told what to do. Others find their own path but Will needed to be told. He was deeply impacted by sharing in a group and came away from his first meeting in tears. Soon, the faith of his Irish Catholic upbringing came back to him and prayer became a regular feature of his life. A moment of realization dawned when he had been abstinent for three months and was facing a court case for crimes he had committed previously. Jason was able to stand up in court and vouch for his transformed character. He spoke of him in glowing terms. For the first time, Will could see his own progress. For the first time there was hope. He soon decided he would train to become a chef. He now works in a top restaurant and lives a happy life on his own boat.

The Dangers

There are, however, some dangers in the connections we are likely to form during recovery. Romantic partnerships are a big potential problem in early recovery. A strange thing happens during early recovery whereby the person engaging in the process begins to look radiant. They become attractive. This is a very common phenomenon. A huge proportion of the romantic relationships that are started during recovery begin very early, break down very quickly and cause great strain on all those involved. So why is it dangerous? Well, relationships require a degree of flexibility, in that you accommodate your lifestyle to your partner. A partner may be unwilling to stay away from bars for instance while for you, this is an essential early recovery behavior. The truth is, your recovery is not their problem. They are well within their rights to reject your recovery lifestyle, and refuse to be part of it. Compromising on recovery for the sake of a relationship is the most natural position to take, and potentially disastrous.

John had drunk all his life. Then he discovered psychedelic drugs, then heroin. Finally, he was mixing prescription opiates with vodka. Like Jason, he was using alcohol to come round from drugs. John quit drink and drugs and was beginning to flourish. He became radiant and attractive. As often happens at this point, as his life came back together, he met someone and started dating. However, this woman was seeing another man at the same time, who soon became extremely upset. Before long the woman's other lover was found dead having hung himself in despair. John was devastated and was thinking, "I need a drink." He came to Jason for help. Jason went with John to the funeral of the man, where they prayed together about this whole sorry state of affairs. John severed his relationship with the woman and explored the Christian faith via an Alpha course. To this day he has not gone back to drink or drugs and now works to help others find recovery.

John, in the example above, survived this particularly severe relationship knock. But many do not, and extreme caution is needed.

Task: The French philosopher Blaise Pascal once said: "All of humanity's problems stem from man's inability to sit quietly in a room alone." See if you can do that now for 10 minutes. Sit with your arms stretched out in front of you. In the first 5 minutes hold your palms downwards and mentally let go of all your burdens, letting them drop to the floor beneath. In the second 5 minutes, hold your palms up as though expecting to receive a gift—and do just that, begin to expect some divine presence or assistance to come to you.

Task: As with your loving actions, make a regular habit of experimenting with ways of being quiet, or praying or meditating.

Further Reading:

Psalm 46:10

Maggie Ross, *Silence: A User's Guide. Vol.1:Process* (London: DLT, 2014)

5

PUT DOWN THE LIES

The Power of Beliefs

IT IS AMAZING HOW, when you roll back an addiction, you uncover what it was masking. There may be a seething mass of insecurities and fears that we had been trying to deal with the wrong way. These now need to be tackled head on.

In all of us there are deep seated beliefs, beliefs that are rooted so deeply that they absolutely define the ways we look at the world. Probably most of these are harmless but the chances are there will be one or two that are not very helpful, yet because they are so deeply rooted they stick around.

Ben's rather lonely and sad childhood had a big effect on him despite there being, deeper still, an originally very sunny outlook on life that made him an exceptionally jolly (and fat) little toddler. Starting school put the dampeners on that. The sunniness was still there deep down but the loneliness of school had a lingering effect. He says it is summed up by the phrase: "I'm abandoned. I'm alone." The anxiety that comes from that has to be countered with something that's true. He has had to work at changing the mantra by meditating deeply on all of the "I am with you" passages from the Bible. The effect on his self-confidence has been decisive.

Another example some of us might face is the kind of deep-seated belief that results from bad behavior itself: the feeling of shame that results. It involves taking the thought "*What I have been doing* is awful and worthless," and changing it into the thought "*I am* awful and worthless," which is a lie. Through deep prayer and meditation, we gain insight after insight that changes our thinking about such things. Jason often says that the recovery journey is a journey of insight through hindsight leading to foresight.

Many beliefs are imbided by osmosis from our culture. One of the commonest ideas we get from our culture is: "You don't have to put up with this! Go on, treat yourself." Other cultures generally have far higher tolerance thresholds than ours for the discomforts or inconveniences of life.

Enough is Enough!

In the first two steps we faced up to what it is we are dealing with and that it is too strong for us. In the third and fourth steps, we accessed new sources of power, power that would be great enough to overcome the big fat hairy bear rearing up at us. Now, with the newly discovered powers of the deep mind and its connection to God, a way is opened to gain insight into the root causes of what we do. To do this well will probably involve these three things:

1. *Be ruthlessly honest with yourself.* Ask yourself: why do I act like this? But don't stop there. Keep asking 'why?' until you get to the baseline rock-bottom, fundamental reason why. Look for clues in any early experiences that threw you off course the most. Ask yourself what sort of lines the culture has fed you over the years that have created a core value within you.

2. *Accept that this will probably take time.* In a minority of cases, the transformation is instantaneous. In most cases there is a process which can take years but eventually this change in your beliefs will be strong enough to sustain your abstinence permanently and effortlessly.

3. *Find ways of building up a stronger sense of self.* The key to fully and finally mastering a nasty habit is to grow out of it. Personal growth into higher levels of maturity will take you through the stages first of subordinating desires for relationships, and then of revising your core beliefs and values. Then, as we will see, there is work to be done in freeing ourselves from unhealthy social pressures as we grow in the ability to unconditionally accept ourselves.

Pause for Thought: Is there an event in your life that rocked your world so much that you were never the same again? In what ways did it change your thinking?

Daniel often describes how impatient he used to be while addicted. He was very easily agitated. Once, he even bashed his head on the floor in a fit of rage because he thought he had lost his passport. He shouted at his friends and family, and screamed at himself over his stupidity. This went on for about ten minutes before it occurred to him that it might not be lost, but simply not where he thought it was. Eventually he discovered it in a different jacket. He still has a scar on his head. Thankfully, these days Daniel is very calm about most things.

The Wisdom of Epictetus

"It is not events that disturb people, it is their judgments concerning them."[1]

So, what made us so disturbable? How did we get ourselves in such a state? There is great wisdom in this saying from the Greek philosopher Epictetus that I have quoted above. In fact this one saying is the basis for the whole system of psychotherapy called Rational, Emotive, Behavioral Therapy, which has been used in the SMART recovery program. The idea is simple: it's not what people say, it's what you believe about what they say that destroys you. It's not the situation, it's what you take that situation to imply about your value as a person that gets to you. A bad day at the office does not, of itself, have the power to make anyone "stressed." There is, in fact, no such thing as a high stress job, or a stressful period of your life. Stress is entirely created by what we believe about what is happening.

So here's the thing: there is no direct route from a bad day to reaching for something harmful, or from a comment you didn't like to lapsing back into an old habit. A leads to C only via B, and B is Belief. We could say A is something like "Activating Incident," and C is "Consequence." The kinds of beliefs that lead to an unhelpful "C" tend to be unreasonable or irrational in some way. They involve putting two and two together and making five. They involve a catastrophic set of conclusions that lead to a feeling that you "just can't stand it!" We "awfulize," "horriblize," and

1. Epictetus, *Enchiridion* 5. Trans. Robert Dobbin, 223.

"catastrophize" things, and answer these awfulnesses with musts, shoulds and oughts that further compound our inability to unconditionally accept ourselves, others and the discomforts of life.[2] This is not to say that you are not entitled to feel deeply sad about something that truly is saddening, or be concerned about something that is a serious concern. The issue is that too often we are needlessly depressed or worried or raging inside and it is helpful to be reminded that we alone got ourselves into that state.

And this applies as much to events in the dim and distant past as it does to things in the present. It is humbling to realize that a great many times in our lives we have felt hurt by people quite needlessly. We, quite literally, believed the worst. We misunderstood. Some of the angriest people we have ever met have also been among the most prone to twisted recollections of events. They have a distorted lens on life and they keep on believing things that aren't true. And all of this anger and frustration—no matter how baseless—has to go somewhere. Very often we don't want to hurt people with the way we feel so we store it up and try to deal with it by ourselves. That's when the problems start. That is where addictions root themselves, and that is where the cracks in relationships start to form.

So, remember, things don't automatically lead to an addictive behavior, they get there only via belief. It is what you have believed that makes you do what you do. A leads to C only via B.

Derek Steele's story is especially shocking. As a child of 7 or 8 he was locked in his room for 30 days as punishment for steeling some sweets. His screaming and banging turned to despair. He was given food but soon could no longer even tell the difference between day and night. He recalls the moment when the thought came: "I must be absolutely worthless." His mother's boyfriend had done the deed but his mother did nothing to rescue him. The pain brought by this sense of worthlessness

---

2. See Ellis & MacLaren, *Rational Emotive Behavior Therapy*, 32–33. See also: http://www.smartrecovery.org.uk/about/

led to him taking his first drugs at the age of 10. Marijuana led to Ecstasy. By the age of 20, Derek had become a liar and a thief as well as a drug addict and alcoholic before checking himself into a Christian rehab. While there he handed his life over to God and got free over the course of a year. On leaving the rehab, he got married and soon started a landscape design business that became hugely successful. After 5 years, he sold it and became an instant millionaire. However, he had been slowly drifting away from God and this moment of selling the business, after the initial euphoria, brought severe despair and a strong desire to either go back to drink or commit suicide. It was then that he heard a quiet voice urging him to call his sponsor who was then able to help him through. He made a renewed commitment and began to volunteer at the Christian rehab where he had stayed all those years before.

Retold in Derek Steele, *Addicted at 10: How I Overcame Addiction, Poverty, and Homelessness to Become a Millionaire by 35* (Austin, TX: Synergy, 2010).

Neil Anderson's course, *Freedom in Christ*, suggests that every participant uses a 'Stronghold Buster' for dealing with the lies they have believed. A Stronghold Buster is a statement that you write out for yourself along the lines of: "I renounce the lie that . . . I announce the truth that . . ." The idea is that you say this statement to yourself every day for about five weeks. Ben has gone through this course twice and he and his wife have even hosted one in their home but Ben was always skeptical of this part. It seemed like an awful lot of hard work, saying the same thing to yourself every day. Then he learned a few things about neuroscience and this thing called "neuroplasticity." Neuroplasticity means that your brain, with enough help from you re-programming it, can literally change shape. Physical changes take place in certain regions of your brain as it accommodates new and different ways of thinking. And when you say your stronghold buster, try saying it forcefully. Some psychotherapists encourage their clients to raise their voice a little as they dispute the lies they have believed. You may find that just one week of forcefully renouncing and announcing has a dramatic effect.

Task: Take the wisdom of Epictetus into your week: It is not things (or comments or people or circumstances) that disturb us but what we take those things to be.

Task: Try writing a simple stronghold buster that deals with one of the root causes of your addiction.

Further Reading:

John 8:31–32

Albert Ellis and Emmett Velten, *When AA Doesn't Work for You: Rational Steps to Quitting Alcohol* (Fort Lee, NJ: Barricade Books, 1992)

Neil Anderson and Steve Goss, *Freedom in Christ* (Guildford: Monarch, 2009)

6

INVESTIGATE THE URGES

You may have quit your bad behavior. For a while, all will be well but quite soon you will experience some powerful urges. These are your friends. These urges, perhaps for the first time, will allow you to understand what forces were driving your behavior all along. When you were stuck in your habit you acted almost without thinking. It was an ingrained habit. It is only now that you have taken a stand against it, that you will experience some very specific triggers that set it off.

So here, we are moving from an understanding of the causes of our behavior—the historic reasons why we do what we do—to the on-going triggers. So there are causes (historic), and there are triggers (on-going). Triggers, in turn, fall into three different kinds, as far as we can tell. There are circumstantial triggers, environmental triggers and mental triggers.

1. *Circumstantial Triggers.* By circumstantial triggers we mean the pressures you face, the feeling that you are not getting enough "me time," the feeling that others are in control and you are at their behest—perhaps you are always walking on eggshells never knowing when you partner or boss is going to have their next meltdown. You feel like you want to have more control over the situation and you feel helpless. You are always worried. Persistent loneliness or boredom can also be a circumstantial trigger. Such circumstances are the general conditions that make lapsing into a bad habit more likely than if your circumstances were better. But such circumstantial factors are only a risk to you because of the wrong kind of coping skills that you have learned over time. With new coping skills you become less vulnerable.

2. *Environmental Triggers.* Environmental triggers can be those simple but powerful moments like walking past the liquor store or the betting shop, being home alone with the internet, or bumping into someone that can sell you drugs. Even if you are not suffering any circumstantial pressures, these factors can drag you back.

3. *Mental Triggers.* Finally, mental triggers are what happens at the moment an urge looms so large in your mind that resisting it seems impossible. At such times there is typically no more than a few seconds to spare before intervening becomes

almost futile. It is a moment known as "euphoric recall," a split second moment of powerfully remembering the pleasure of the habit and completely forgetting the pain that resulted.

This was all a lot to take in so we will go through these in slower time below.

A Closer Look at Circumstantial Triggers

Often, it is high social expectations, or some other social pressure, that cause us to feel that various external pressures are in control. In response, we try to wrest back control, we try to take affirmative action, take matters into our own hands. The urges are always preceded by strong feelings of helplessness. The harmful thing we end up doing is a way, paradoxically, of taking control (even though the behavior itself is quite seriously out of control). The exact nature of the behavior is only the outward form of it. At its heart is the inability to cope with some form of pressure that leaves us feeling hopeless and helpless—and rebellious. And there is always a reasonably long lead-in before we reach that point when we "know" we are going to do that thing again. There is always the opportunity, as we will explore further below, to deconstruct the feelings and thoughts before they lead to a sudden surge of the will.

The Anatomy of an Urge

The following is mainly inspired by Lance Dodes' work in this area:[1]

- Every relapse is preceded by a feeling of helplessness.
- There is a mounting feeling of frustration about not feeling in control of your own mind and life. Something or someone else is calling all the shots.

---

1. See his home page: http://www.lancedodes.com/a-new-treatment-approach/[accessed 21/05/2015].

- As soon as the opportunity arises, this frustration is expressed in a substitute action—a displacement—rather than dealing directly with the helplessness. You take affirmative action that gives you back control. In reality it is a splurge, a blow-out, a crash-and-burn episode which brings only regret.

- Your feelings of regret then lead to self-downing, leaving you even more vulnerable to addictive behaviors in an effort to self-soothe.

Lance Dodes gives a description of one of his clients. He was a very hard working individual who pushed himself to achieve more and more but then found that he was drinking heavily without being aware of the reason. When he began to see that his drinking always followed times when he didn't allow himself to relax, and to notice how much it enraged him to lose his own time for himself, he could see that his drinking was far from an inexplicable act. He could see that when he drank he expressed his fury at being out of control of his time and his life, and that he took back a sense of power over his life by doing something that was just for him. Once he understood this dynamic, he could take action to prevent the sudden urge to drink. He decided to be easier on himself and take more care to carve out time for himself in his busy schedule.

Urges are a malfunction of the will. At the moment they occur they seem to utterly bypass the rationality and cause us to act against our better judgment. In reality they are the end result of a process of resenting things and feeling helpless.

Karen Rabbitt's story is a striking example both of the power of expectations, and also of the power of self-acceptance. She was a newly qualified Christian therapist who felt that she was out of her depth. She already struggled with the fact that she was a professional from a working class background but now, a married couple whose marriage she had been trying to save was seeking a divorce. Her feelings of shame and failure were deepening. Her self-talk was: "Aren't you getting too big for your britches?" Her way of coping with these low feelings and thoughts was to eat lots of chocolate. Her favorite thing was choc chip cookies, which she would bake herself, and then eat as many as six or seven in a single sitting. Her love of sugar and fat were taking the edge off her feelings of anxiety and inadequacy. As she steadily piled on the weight and felt herself losing control of her behavior, the self-punishing thoughts came: "When you're seeing your clients, you act like you have everything under control, but your eating is out of control. You're going to be a fat slob. You know better." She describes how she soon found herself in a classic addiction cycle: feeling shame, eating to deal with the shame, then feeling even more shame because of the over-eating, and dealing with that in turn by eating more chocolate. Compared to heroin or crack this addiction might seem trivial but, in fact, it would soon become just as life threatening as a narcotics addiction. The real breakthrough came when she learned to listen to what she calls a "kinder voice" than the self-punishing voice: "You can love your overweight self, just as you are, because Jesus does. Even if you're a food addict." This helped her to stop gaining weight and be happy with her "matronly" figure. She also began to take regular exercise. However, it was not until the doctor told her that her triglyceride levels were so high she was at imminent risk of a heart attack that she finally cut out the sugar and fat and her weight began to return to a size 10. But she is clear that without coming to that point of self-acceptance, none of that would have been possible, even with the health scare.

Her story is told here: http://www.todayschristian-woman.com/articles/2007/january/i-was-food-addict.html [accessed 22/5/2015].

The crucial insight when it comes to dealing with circumstantial triggers is that the urge you feel is a misdirected but otherwise

BEYOND THIS DARKNESS

healthy and normal desire to take control of a situation that is making you feel out of control. Dodes calls it a "displacement."[2]

Pause for Thought: Take some time now to think about times when feelings of helplessness made you say, "To hell with it" and you went and did that thing again. Obviously, you recognize in hindsight that your chosen course of action did nothing to remedy the situation. List some things that you wish you had done that would have been much more helpful.

Now read Romans 12:2. Here's the rub: *You will not be transformed for as long as you are conformed.* For some of us conformity to social expectation is the single biggest reason why there is no transformation. In a sense, my advice here goes against the earlier stage where we gave up our bad behavior for the sake of a relationship. The difference here is that whereas that decision was made out of love, this habit of mind is all about fear. This is about your fear of what people think of you, not your love for them. But you don't need their approval. You have survived the absence of it before; you can survive it again if you need to. Your life does not depend upon everybody liking you or accepting you. You have a Rock on which to stand. Find relief from the counterproductive pressures you face in the fact that you are the person God made you to be.

Pause for Thought: What circumstances do you struggle with at present? What was the most recent occasion when these circumstances led to a lapse?

A Closer Look at Environmental Triggers

Environmental triggers are those times when you had not been conscious of a desire to go back to your habit until suddenly

2. E.g. Dodes, *Heart of Addiction*, 6–7.

confronted with an opportunity to do it. The very best solution, of course, is quarantine. It will be about three months before you can be exposed to this kind of trigger and not feel a craving. One alcoholic was recommended a six month stay at a lockdown rehab by her doctor. Only then could she be sure that, once she was back out in the real world, she could walk past the liquor store and not succumb.[3] However, few of us have the luxury of withdrawing from the world. Mostly we must find ways of dealing with those times when, inevitably, we will be left alone with the thing we used to love. And it will be singing its sweetest song, and it will be assuring us that just once won't hurt.

However, environmental triggers can also include negative triggers, what are called contra-suggestion. These are often generated by rules, whether our own or those imposed upon us that were meant to help. You may discover that it is your most determined efforts at constraining your own behavior that can be the very thing that sets it off.

Consider the film *Meet the Parents*. Ben Stiller stars as the hapless fiancée of a girl whose father, played by Robert De Niro, is a retired CIA agent, complete with his own lie detector and other sophisticated ways of spying on and controlling the behavior of this thoroughly intimidated son-in-law to be. This man clearly had no hope of ever fully pleasing this highly protective custodian of propriety and decency. Needless to say, it was precisely in this kind of environment that the young man's behavior spiraled out of control. He was trying too hard to please in the face of impossible odds. One terrible accident and misunderstanding after the other confirmed and reconfirmed all of the father's worst fears about this man. In the end, only the girl's determination to marry him won the day.

And our point is that this sort of thing can happen despite the fact that we want to please. There is "another law" at work within us, as Paul says (Romans 7:21). It is like harboring a terror cell. Terror cells can lurk successfully within a nation that is otherwise

---

3. Weeks. "Only Lockdown Rehab Worked," https://www.thefix.com/content/only-lockdown-rehab-worked [accessed 29 January 2017].

on friendly terms with the nation being attacked. Such was the case during the Northern Ireland conflict. Berty Ahern was on good terms with Tony Blair, yet lurking within Ireland's shores were people for whom the political processes of compromise had not gone nearly far enough.

Paul sums it up in a most profound statement: "The strength of sin is the law." (1Cor15:56). This thing inside us, this terror cell, can mean that the very effort to do what is right can be the catalyst that makes our behavior spiral out of control. It is, by nature, rebellious and rebellion needs something to rebel against. It needs a law so that it can break it, a New Year's resolution so that it can transgress it, a sky high expectation so that it can kick against it. There is a place for quarantining yourself: making sure that you do not come into contact with temptation for a season but it is important to watch for the way that any constraints you place on yourself might actually end up making matters worse. Take away the laws, the resolutions, the fearful expectations, the self-effort, and the terror cell goes to sleep. Once it is fast asleep, the Spirit can then come and give us a whole new set of urges and desires.

Pause for Thought: Is there something you can do to give yourself some distance from your temptation? Can you change the settings on your internet? Can you go home a different route?

A Closer Look at Mental Triggers

Mental triggers are memories. That is all. They are nothing but harmless memories. Something, usually the thing you are starting to crave, reminds you of pleasures past and, at that moment, you are unable to remember the pain. We call this euphoric recall. It can involve something not directly related to the habit: a smell, a word, a phrase, a piece of music. It will often take us by surprise and prove nearly impossible to resist. We might find that we are able to fight it off initially but, within moments, the feeling is back, only stronger and reinforced with all sorts of reasons why, based on your circumstances, you really deserve it this time. Basically, it will keep knocking until we let it in. So, back to the question then: if we cannot realistically withdraw from the world for 3–6 months until the power of euphoric recall subsides, then what must we do?

There is an unforgettable moment in the sci-fi movie *Divergent*. Beatrice Prior, the protagonist, played by Shailene Woodley, is classed as a divergent because she is gifted with having abilities of many different kinds. She can think on a number of different levels. Unlike almost everyone else, she can be selfless, peaceful, honest, brave and intellectual all at the same time. Before she was discovered to be a divergent, she needed to be tested, just like everyone else was once they reached a certain age, so that they could enter the work force and be given the right job to do. The test involved being subjected to a disturbing experience in which she is drugged into a dreamlike state. While drugged she finds herself in a world generated by her imagination but which seems power-fully real and her every choice within this imaginary dreamscape is monitored by an examiner. She finds herself confronted with all kinds of problems and terrifying dangers such as mad dogs. The way she reacts will determine what type she falls into. At one point in her dreamlike world she is trapped in a glass tank filled with water. She cannot breathe. However, instead of being terrified she uses the combined power of all her special qualities. The power of her mind proves so great that she is, quite literally, able to think outside the box. She calmly says to herself, "This isn't real." At that point, all it takes is for one of her fingers to lightly tap the glass and it starts to crack. She taps again and it shatters.

We could also think of Jesus in the wilderness being tempted by the devil. He knows he must fast from food for this test but he has become extremely hungry. He sees some desert rocks which remind him of loaves of fresh bread. He can almost smell them. The devil says to him, "Go on. If you are the Son of God, command these stones to become bread." The devil soon realizes what he is up against, however. Like Breatice Prior, he has a simple phrase up his sleeve, which he quietly says: "It is written, 'Man cannot live on bread alone but by every word that comes from the mouth of God."

What we all need is a simple phrase which works for us. If you are a sexual fantasist, you might find that exact phrase of Beatrice Prior is all it takes to break the spell of the fantasy before it gets going: "This isn't real." A phrase that helps you to remember the madness might help if you are tempted to drink, overeat or use a drug, a phrase such as: "Then what?" If you have been a gambler and have taken steps to "Put off" the gambling behavior and "put on" something else which requires you to save up some money, say, "I'm saving up for. . ."

Brother Lawrence was a French monk who worked in a busy monastery kitchen but he found that he could continuously enjoy a strong sense of God's presence all through the day, even in the midst of the noise and clamor of the kitchen. Sometimes, though, he did find that his heart would drift away from that intimate fellowship with God. At such times he would use a simple phrase such as: "My God, here I am, all yours," or "Lord, fashion me according to thy heart."[4] Immediately he was back in that sense of the nearness of God which he loved so much. You might like to try one of Lawrence's phrases when you can feel yourself drifting off into an internet search that you already know isn't going to take you anywhere good.

4. Lawrence, *The Practice of the Presence of God*, 35–36.

Pause for Thought: Next time temptation comes knocking hard at your door, what would you like to say to it? Try writing that down.

To Sum Up: The next time circumstantial pressures build up, let them find you having already got some good habits in place that diffuse those pressures in the *right* way. The next time you are unavoidably in an environment that you know is risky, be on your guard and call upon the Lord. The next time you experience the mental trigger of a euphoric recall, may you be armed with a simple phrase that completely defeats it. And do take comfort in the thought that this fight will not be endless. You will get to the point where you will have a much less distorted memory, one that includes the pain as well as the pleasure, and resisting temptation will not be nearly so tough.

Prayer:

> *The whole of me lives beneath the reign of grace and the inside of me is infused with your powerful Holy Spirit.*
>
> *And so I rest today in the knowledge that no demand can be made of me that I'm required by You, but not empowered by You, to fulfil.*
>
> *Today, I have nothing to rebel against so my rebellion sleeps.*
>
> *Today, I have nothing against You for Your goodness has led me to repentance.*
>
> *Today, may I know the mind of Your Spirit.*
>
> *Today, may the law of the Spirit of life in Christ keep me free. Amen*

Further Reading:

Romans 12:2

Romans 6:14

Lance Dodes, *The Heart of Addiction* (New York: HarperCollins, 2003)

7

TAKE THE OUT TRACK

LET'S SUMMARIZE WHERE THE STAMP-IT-OUT program has got us to so far:

1. Step back by understanding that it's not you.

2. Take stock by accepting the scale of the problem.

3. Acquire a new Master by loving God instead of your addiction.

4. Make deep connections with God and others.

5. Put down the lies you have believed so that you are less disturbable.

6. Investigate your urges and learn to deal with pressures in a more direct way.

7. Take the OUT Relapse and Recovery Maintenance Program: Overcoming self-hate, Uniting yourself to the Master, and Trailing the Spirit.

So, having gone through the first six steps, you are now what we might call an OUT Patient. You are about to take the OUT program. You will probably need to revisit steps 5 and 6 a few times and Step 4 is a lifestyle commitment but you have now got the essential foundations in place. However, the truth is you have almost certainly had a wobble by now. It may have been a lapse—a momentary stumble but with a quick recovery; or it may have been a relapse—a stumble from which you did not recover and you feel like you are virtually back where you started. The thing you need to know is how to fail well, and this is what the OUT Track is all about. You need to be able to learn all you can from failures and recover quickly. The problem is not slipping up—we all do that—the problem is staying there and not getting up, not getting OUT.

So here are some pointers about how to get up. These are also good tools for maintaining and improving a state of recovery. You can go over them again and again. They are based on Romans 8:1–2. There we find three things: "no condemnation," "in Christ," and the "law of the Spirit." We can picture these as three steps as follows:

1. Overcome Self-Hate.

This is a big one. Ben vividly remembers an alcoholic who had re-lapsed and had come to visit him at his house. His gut-wrenching words as he walked away that evening were: "I hate myself, Ben. I hate myself." Thankfully he did stay on the path to recovery and things have got better since but he still struggles. "I fought pound-ing waves of regret and guilt," says one former porn addict, "I felt a million miles from good, a billion light years from God."[1] It is quite common for porn addicts to feel unable to accept or receive the love of God despite knowing all about it: "I began to question the ability of God's love to extend to me," says one, ". . . I understood grace, unconditional compassion, mercy beyond understanding; but I started to wonder if I was the exception clause, the one that God had abandoned."[2]

Here are some marvelous statements from Paul, which can be written onto your heart perhaps by being repeated like a mantra using one of the meditative techniques like those suggested in Step 4, or made into part of a stronghold buster like in Step 5: "For all have sinned and all fall short of the glory of God, and are justi-fied freely by his grace . . . Therefore having been justified by faith we have peace with God through our Lord Jesus Christ . . . God demonstrates his own love towards us in that while we were still sinners Christ died for us . . . There is therefore now no condem-nation to those who are in Christ." In fact, you can see how these statements could go together to form one big statement. They are definitely worth at least putting up on a wall somewhere.

To be justified means that it is just-as-if-ied never sinned. It is just as if you had never done anything shameful. God is able to completely accept you and bless you with rewards you haven't earned. He does this for the simple reason that you are in Christ and Christ *has* earned them. God is able to love you just for who

1. Groves, "I'm a Christian Addicted to Porn." *Christianity Today* [accessed online 1 Nov 2016] http://www.christianitytoday.com/iyf/truelifestories/ithappenedtome/im-christian-addicted-to-porn.html?start=1

2. Anon., "My Story," *TechMission*. Accessed online 1 Nov 2016: http://www.safefamilies.org/recoverystories.php

you are, without allowing the things you have done to define you because the things Christ has done have covered over those things.

Daniel has got the place where he is not at all tortured by the things he has done or said. As you will have seen from this book, he is able to be open about his entire past. There is nothing keeping him awake at night. At last he feels like a genuine person, not hiding anything. But how do we get to this place of peace when we've blown it? Supposing you relapse in a really major way: the feelings of shame and self-loathing will be intense and very hard to shift. They will hang about you like a millstone, and if we don't get rid of them they will become the thing that guarantees we will mess up again, and then again. Before we know it we will be almost back where we were. This is how guilt operates. There is something very self-destructive about it. It generates more of the very thing that led to the guilty feelings in the first place. This is because the easiest way to anaesthetize the pain of failure is to fail again, only more outrageously than before, and then again. It won't feel as bad the second time. By the third occasion your conscience will have gone nicely to sleep.

But there is a better way: "If we walk in the light as he is in the light we have fellowship with one another and the blood of Jesus his Son cleanses us from all sin." We have sinned and we need to admit it. Like those bravely approaching the 5th Step on AA, we need to "admit the exact nature of our wrongs." Jason describes how some people are willing to engage with this process most of the way but there is what he describes as a five per cent that they hold back. There is a zone of secrecy which they share with no one, and this can make all the difference to the likelihood of sustaining a full and joyful recovery.

If you have someone that you trust enough with your secrets, tell them the exact nature of your wrongs. But whether you have a special someone like that or not, you must tell these things to God: the exact nature of them with no generalizations and no blaming of other people or your circumstances. It is then that you will experience his forgiving grace washing over you and you won't feel like repeating your wrongs.

Statement: *Though what I have done is worthless and dirty, I have no right to hate that which God has demonstrated that he loves. I admit the exact nature of my wrongs and accept the forgiveness freely offered to me.*

Task: If you have lapsed, take a journal or notebook, open it, and ask yourself three questions:

1. What did I do?

2. What were the reasons? Do some more work around Step 5

3. What were the triggers? Do some more work around Step 6

Now write down your insights in your journal and close it. When you have done that, it is time to stop the post mortem and move on. If you continue to get feelings of self-loathing say, "There is no condemnation to those who are in Christ Jesus."

2. Unite Yourself to the Master.

There is a certain feeling of loss involved when transitioning from addiction to recovery. The once trusted supports against fear and hurt are no longer an option. If your very identity was once bound up with the addictive behavior, it is natural to struggle to find an identity or meaning in anything else. The transition to recovery can potentially impact every relationship, every activity, every location and every situation that you were once so at home with. It is important to be reminded that there is a lot more to recovery than merely stopping or unlearning the addictive behavior. In AA there is what is known derisively as the 1–2–3 Merry-go-Round. It is life stuck at the first three of the twelve steps but not really mastering even these. People stuck there are called dry drunks. It is a miserable life in which the old sources of comfort are gone but the old way of thinking remains.

The important thing to do then, once you have overcome self-hate, is to affirm again to yourself, your body and your new Master, that you have changed sides in this conflict. You are now in union with Christ but this is not a union between two mates but a union with your Lord. It is not a union of equals—thankfully! Jesus does not only enter into your pain and feel it with you, he places his scepter over it, he reigns over it.

To enter into the benefit of that union and to experience again his mastery over all the things you do that you hate, you need to submit to his Lordship. Paul talks about presenting our bodies to God, or presenting the members of our body as "weapons for doing right." Ben regularly does what the Apostle Paul says we should do. Whenever no-one is looking, and even sometimes when everyone is looking, he quite literally stands or kneels with uplifted arms and presents himself as belonging wholly to God and ready for service. Bill W in the Big Book talks about one man who would kick his slippers under the bed to make himself kneel down to retrieve them. While kneeling he prayed.

You may need to keep on presenting yourself to the new Master, even in the face of continued moral slippage and very imperfect resistance to temptation. Just keep confessing the exact nature of your wrongs (Step 1 of the OUT Track) and keep presenting your body (Step 2 of the OUT Track).

Statement: *I present my body to my new Master in unreserved readiness to obey him and I declare that I am free from my old master.*

Task: memorize at least one of these passages today: Romans 6:2, 6, 12–13, 16, 19. Make it your goal to memorize them all.

3. Trail the Spirit.

Remember how we looked at Jack Trimpey's ideas about the Addictive Voice. Paul would have called this the voice of the flesh, and it is opposed to the voice of the Spirit. I think this is what he means when he says, "The law of the Spirit of life in Christ has made you free from the law of sin and death" (Rom.8:2). This law is a governing principle, like the law of gravity. You can rely on it and you should listen to it. If I did not heed the "voice," as it were, of the law of gravity, I would step off cliffs and buildings believing I would gently float down or fly. I listen to it by remembering what it was like to transgress it. I subconsciously remember the lessons learned from early childhood when I would have fallen over and hurt myself countless times while I learned the hard way that the law of gravity cannot be transgressed. Jason always says you have to "stay close to the madness." You have to keep remembering the pain of your lowest moments in the addiction and not listen to that other voice that only reminds you of the fun you had.

But you can trust the Spirit in you. You will discover him working. You will discover him leading you and filling you with joy and peace. You will also notice him giving you new urges and desires to do new things.

Daniel's first sponsor in a 12 step program found great purpose in painting pictures, as well as by helping out at his 12 step group. Others go into education and learn subjects of interest, or start a business. One even went on to become a stand-up comedian. Perhaps the Spirit has given you a clear picture in your mind regarding what you want to do. Michael Vlach is clear that gambling addicts must not only "put off" the old habits and haunts but must "put on" something new: some new activity to fill the time once used up on gambling (Col. 3:8–14).[3]

Many, however, continue to suffer from a great lack of motivation and hope for the future. If this is you, start by developing a routine that enables you to truly connect with God—Step 4 again.

---

3. Vlach, "The Put Off, Put On Principle." Accessed online 1 Nov 2016: http://www.chancetochange.org/files/chance_to_change.pdf

This will naturally encourage passion and motivation to truly experience life. If your routine isn't satisfying, try to find one that is. The drive that Daniel has in his life now has been the result of forcing himself to do things he has not wanted to do. All of this culminated in him finding purpose, and an identity as a recovered person. This is the desired outcome of recovery: a life positively flourishing without the addiction.

———————————————

Caleb was a heroin addict who first came to Jason's recovery group in a wheelchair. His legs had been crushed by having jumped off a sixty foot high bridge in a failed suicide attempt. He had been told he would never walk again. In no time at all, while in a residential rehab, Caleb was out of his wheelchair and helping to sand the floor, sliding around on his bottom. Within four months, he had exchanged his wheelchair for crutches, and became extremely adept at getting around on them. Within nine months he got rid of his crutches and decided he wanted to be a mechanic. He got a job repairing London taxi cabs and today he drives articulated lorries for a living. Jason says, "His vision kept him alive." Caleb was driven by a vision of life in which drugs would play no part and in which nothing was ever going to hold him back, not even two shattered legs.

———————————————

Philip had done it all before. He had played the recovery game countless times but was still drinking. He had never got over the constant gnawing, the endless drip-drip of the voice that says, "You know you've got to drink." In the end his breakthrough came when he began to develop a dream in his heart of teaching English as a foreign language. He was captured by a vision, a glimpse of how life could be. He worked night and day to finish his course. Soon he found a job in Spain teaching

English as a foreign language. He now lives a new life in Spain and is in a steady relationship. He is living his dream.

You may not yet feel that you are driven by a vision but it is important to start exploring the possibilities. You can always change your mind. You could try poetry, learn how to cook, do odd jobs and DIY, immerse yourself in music, enjoy walking. The Spirit will involve Himself in this process of finding purpose. Before long you will find yourself trailing His lead as he inspires and excites you with some new venture for your new life.

Statement: *In entering into my union with my Master I have crossed over from living in the flesh to life in the Spirit and I now look for evidences of the Spirit inspiring and leading me into life and peace.*

CONCLUSION

As you continue through recovery, many wonderful changes happen. Life picks up, and the problems of yesterday seem gone for good. Sometimes, you struggle to even remember doing the things you once did. It feels strange to think you were once that person. . . but you were! If you have committed yourself to recovery, your whole self will be changed; your desires, interests, morality, world-view and pleasures will be shaped by God instead of you. Nothing compares to God's ability to transform, and it will prove crucial to keep working towards deeper and deeper connection with Him.

Daniel reminisces that he had never laughed as much as he did through recovery, and this has continued. He has cried with joy on countless occasions. Awful things have happened since recovery but these have not been able disturb him. He still becomes easily overwhelmed by how wonderful his life has become. All these reasons to be cheerful were overlooked during his addiction. In addiction he was never truly alive. He remembers that, as an addict, he was awkward and uncomfortable talking to people, which he would compensate for by being loud and confrontational. He was not comfortable in his own skin, and kept trying to escape, but now he can confidently approach situations which used to cause him great distress, such as public speaking. He is able to be himself both with strangers and friends. He feels free to open up to people, or to choose not to.

Jason, too, is a picture of the end game for anyone pursuing recovery. I (Ben) often see him at church next to his wife lost in worship. Sometimes he seems to be the only one who is completely caught up with God while everyone else seems distracted or inattentive. He has worked in recovery for years helping people, people who can be aggressive and rude, often fail to keep appointments, and often fail to reach a lasting recovery. Most recovery workers burn out by now but Jason is sustained by God.

Vigilance is required, of course, especially when some time has elapsed, and everything seems wonderful. Daniel has found that he tends to rely more and more on his own understandings and can forget to acknowledge God in his daily life. God can start to become an idea, rather than a personal being, and prayer is like going through the motions. This results in him becoming more and more like the man he used to be: easily agitated, not content with his achievements, unhappy with his circumstances, and comparing himself to others. He even starts to blame God for things and connecting with God starts to feel like a chore. This kind of cooling off is likely to happen to any person of faith, though for the former addict, there are added dangers. The worst thing is the process by which you start to forget how bad things were. You forget the madness. Make a point of trying to remember the things you used to do. Don't fall into the trap of believing that it could never happen again, or that if you did choose to indulge in your addiction, you could control it this time around. You are essentially the same person you always were, and you should allow the experiences that shaped your early recovery to shape your life just as much today.

We pray that, by God's almighty power, you may be strengthened with might in your inner being to keep walking the walk filled with His joy.

Ben, Jason, Daniel.

BIBLIOGRAPHY

Amerman, Michelle. "Addiction Is Not You, It's Your Cage." *Pathways* (Sep 23, 2015). Accessed online 28 Feb 2017: http://pathwaysreallife.com/addiction-you-its-cage/

Anon., "My Story," *TechMission*. Accessed online 1 Nov 2016: http://www.safefamilies.org/recoverystories.php

Buker, Bill. "Spiritual Development and the Epistemology of Systems Theory." *Journal of Psychology and Theology* 31:2 (2003),143–153.

Chambers, Maxi. "What I Lost By Gambling." *Today's Christian Woman* (November 1996). Accessed online 28 Feb 2017: http://www.todayschristianwoman.com/articles/1996/november/6w6074.html

Dann, Bucky. *Addiction: Pastoral Responses*. Nashville: Abingdon, 2002.

Dodes, Lance. *The Heart of Addiction*. New York: HarperCollins, 2002.

Ellis, Albert and Catherine MacLaren. *Rational Emotive Behavior Therapy: A Therapist's Guide*. Atascadero, CA: Impact, 2005.

Epictetus. *Enchiridion*. Tr. Robert Dobbin. London: Penguin, 2008.

Fantelli, Charlotte. "Sex, Sex, Sex': The Story of a Female Sex Addict," *Mental Healthy*. Accessed Online 1 Nov 2016: http://www.mentalhealthy.co.uk/news/924-female-sex-addiction.html

Groves, Shaun. "I'm a Christian Addicted to Porn," *Christianity Today* [accessed online 1 Nov 2016] http://www.christianitytoday.com/iyf/truelifestories/ithappenedtome/im-christian-addicted-to-porn.html?start=1

Kegan, Robert. *In Over Our Heads: The Mental Demands of Modern Life*. Cambridge, MA: Harvard University Press, 1994.

———. *The Evolving Self*. Cambridge, MA: Harvard University Press, 1982.

Lawrence of the Resurrection. *The Practice of the Presence of God*. London: Hodder & Stoughton, 1981.

Lenters, William. *The Freedom we Crave*. Grand Rapids: Eerdmans, 1985.

Lewis, C.S. *The Great Divorce*. London: HarperColllins, 2009.

Royce, Richard. "Early Stoicism and Akrasia." *Phronesis* XL:3 (1995), 315–335.

Trimpey, Jack. *Rational Recovery: The New Cure for Substance Addiction*. New York: Pocket Books, 1996.

Bibliography

Vlach, Michael. "Escaping the Lies of Gambling Addiction." *Christianity*. [accessed online 1 Nov 2016] http://www.christianity.com/1289790/

———. "The Put Off, Put On Principle: Christ-Centered Gambling Recovery." Accessed online 1 Nov 2016: http://www.chancetochange.org/files/chance_to_change.pdf

Walsh, Kilian, trans., *The Works of St Bernard of Clairvaux Volume 3: On the Song of Songs II*. London: Mowbray, 1976.

Ward, Benedicta, trans. *The Prayers and Meditations of St Anselm*. London: Penguin, 1973.

Weeks, Maria. "Only Lockdown Rehab Worked." https://www.thefix.com/content/only-lockdown-rehab-worked [accessed 29 January 2017].

Wilson, Bill. *Alcoholics Anonymous: The Story of How Many Thousands of Men and Women Have Recovered from Alcoholism*. New York: Alcoholics Anonymous World Services, 1995.

.